SPACE
MYSTERIES

WHERE
MOON COME FROM?

Gareth Stevens
Publishing

BY MICHAEL PORTMAN

Please visit our website, www.garethstevens.com. For a free color catalog of all our high-quality books, call toll free 1-800-542-2595 or fax 1-877-542-2596.

Library of Congress Cataloging-in-Publication Data

Portman, Michael, 1976-
 Where did the moon come from? / Michael Portman.
     p. cm. — (Space mysteries)
ISBN 978-1-4339-8278-1 (pbk.)
ISBN 978-1-4339-8279-8 (6-pack)
ISBN 978-1-4339-8277-4 (library binding)
1. Moon—Origin—Juvenile literature. I. Title. II. Series: Portman, Michael, 1976- Space mysteries.
 QB582.P67 2013
 523.3—dc23

                                   2012031293

First Edition

Published in 2013 by
Gareth Stevens Publishing
111 East 14th Street, Suite 349
New York, NY 10003

Copyright © 2013 Gareth Stevens Publishing

Designer: Katelyn E. Reynolds
Editor: Therese Shea

Photo credits: Cover, pp. 1, 5 iStockphoto/Thinkstock.com; cover, pp. 1, 3–32 (background texture) David M. Schrader/Shutterstock.com; pp. 3–32 (fun fact graphic) © iStockphoto.com/spxChrome; p. 7 Hemera/Thinkstock.com; pp. 9, 13, 23, 29 NASA; p. 10 StockTrek Images/Thinkstock.com; p. 11 Photos.com/Thinkstock.com; p. 15 StockTrek Images/The Agency Collection/Getty Images; p. 17 Richard Wahlstrom/Stone/Getty Images; p. 19 Fry Design Ltd/Photographer's Choice/Getty Images; p. 21 NASA/Don Davis; p. 25 NYPL NYPL/Photo Researchers/Getty Images; p. 27 StockTrek Images/Getty Images; p. 28 NASA/Regan Geeseman.

Printed in the United States of America

CPSIA compliance information: Batch #CW13GS: For further information contact Gareth Stevens, New York, New York at 1-800-542-2595.

CONTENTS

Words in the glossary appear in **bold** type the first time they are used in the text.

OUR MOON

The moon is Earth's closest neighbor. It outshines everything else in the night sky. Throughout history, the moon has been both a guide and a timekeeper. Some ancient people even thought the moon was a god.

People dreamed of making a journey to the moon. In 1969, that dream came true. Over the course of history, we've learned a lot about the moon, but much still remains a mystery. We're still trying to answer the big question: "Where did the moon come from?"

OUT OF THIS WORLD!

The Romans named their goddess of the moon Luna. That's why we use the word "lunar" to describe things having to do with the moon.

We can't see the moon every night. How much we see depends on the positions of Earth, the moon, and the sun.

5

MANY MOONS

There are at least 146 moons in our **solar system**. A moon is any natural object that circles, or orbits, a planet. Some planets have many moons. Earth has just one. The moon is about 2,160 miles (3,475 km) across. That's about one-fourth the size of Earth.

Since the moon is close to Earth, it can seem bigger than it actually is. The moon appears to be the same size as the sun. The sun is much bigger, but it's also much farther away.

OUT OF THIS WORLD!

The moon doesn't produce its own light. Sunlight bounces off it.

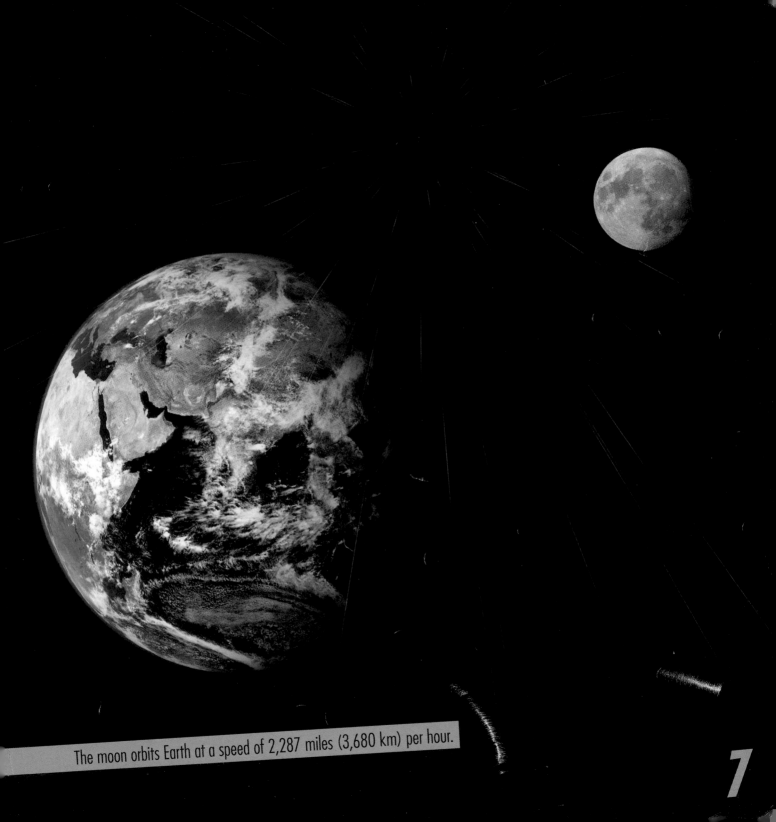

The moon orbits Earth at a speed of 2,287 miles (3,680 km) per hour.

HOLD STEADY

In many ways, Earth depends on the moon. Life as we know it would be much different without it. Because of **gravity**, everything in space is in a constant game of tug-of-war. The moon's gravity pulls on Earth, and Earth's gravity pulls on the moon.

Because Earth isn't perfectly round, it wobbles as it spins, or rotates. The moon's gravity slows Earth's wobble. This has allowed Earth to have comfortable and steady weather.

OUT OF THIS WORLD!

Without the moon, Earth would spin much faster, and the days would be much shorter.

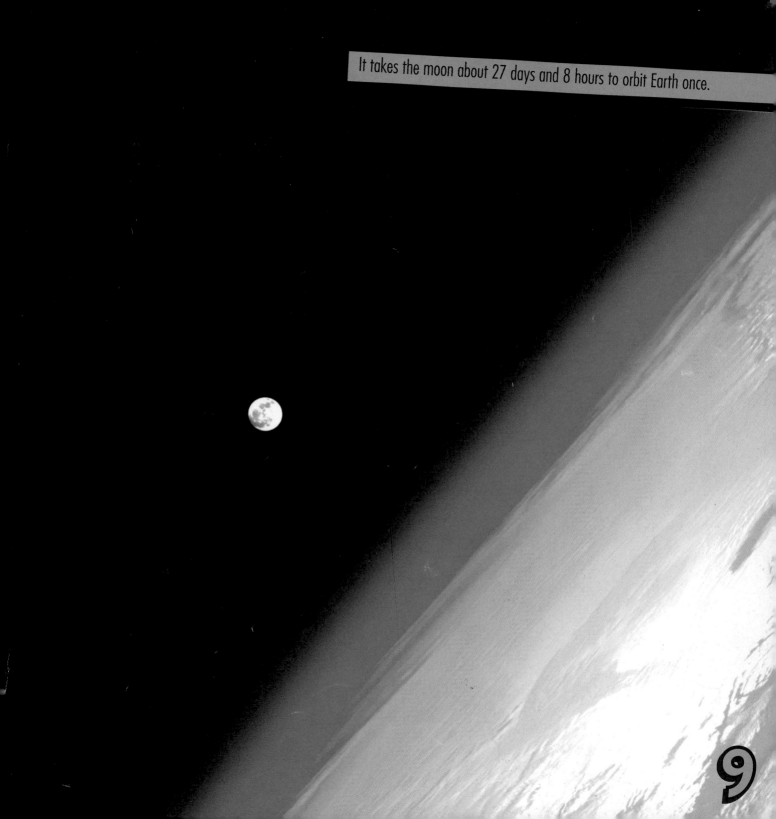

9

EARLY OBSERVATIONS

In ancient times, some people believed the moon was a bowl of fire. Others thought it was a giant mirror. Many thought the moon had oceans—and even life.

In the 1600s, the Italian **astronomer** Galileo was the first person to use a **telescope** to study the moon. During Galileo's time, many people thought the moon was smooth. In 1609, Galileo noted that the moon was covered with mountains and valleys, much like Earth is.

drawings of the moon made by Galileo

Galileo also discovered moons orbiting the planet Jupiter.

SEAS ON THE MOON

When we look at the moon, we see areas of light and dark. Long ago, some people believed the light areas were landmasses and the dark areas were oceans. The light areas are the lunar highlands. The lunar highlands are rocky and covered with bowl-shaped dents called craters.

The dark areas are called maria. *Maria* is the Latin word for "seas." In fact, the lunar maria were once seas of hot liquid, or molten, rock. When the rock cooled, it formed flat, dark areas of rock.

OUT OF THIS WORLD!

Some of the moon's mountain peaks are about 16,000 feet (4,875 m) tall.

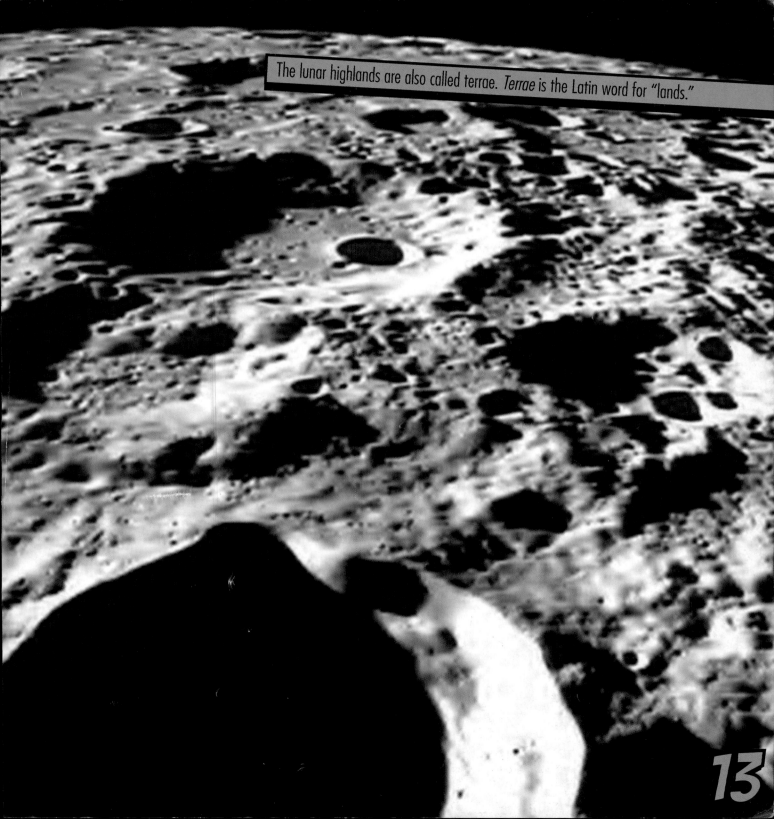

The lunar highlands are also called terrae. *Terrae* is the Latin word for "lands."

13

HOT ROCKS

When the moon was young, much of it was made of molten rock. The rock cooled quickly to form a solid surface. However, for more than a billion years, **lava** continued to pour out of lunar volcanoes. Finally, the volcanoes stopped. All this contributed to the solid surface we see today.

The top layer of the moon is called the crust. Below the crust is a layer called the mantle. At the center of the moon is its core. Scientists believe **magma** is still near the moon's core.

OUT OF THIS WORLD!

For many years, scientists weren't sure what the moon's core was made of. They now think that the moon has a core of solid iron.

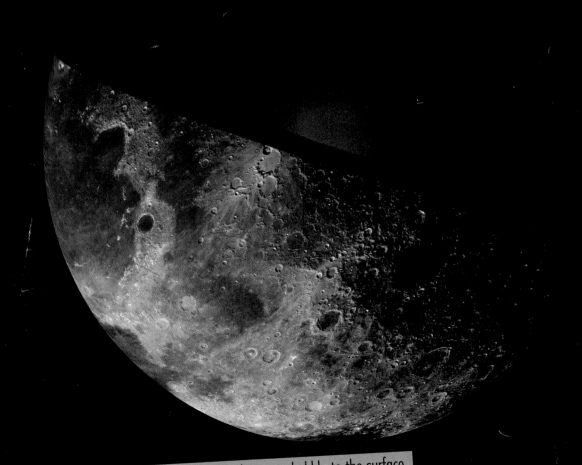

Scientists think the moon's magma is too heavy to bubble to the surface.

SILENT WORLD

A thick layer of gases called the atmosphere surrounds Earth. There's no atmosphere around the moon. There's no lunar wind, rain, or snow. The sky is always black. Without air, sound cannot travel on the moon. The moon is a lifeless, silent place.

Since there's no wind or liquid water on the moon, its surface changes very, very slowly. The moon is covered in a layer of powdery soil and scattered rocks. Dust on the moon can sit in the same place for hundreds of years.

Because there's no atmosphere on the moon, **temperatures** range from very, very hot to very, very cold.

EARLY THEORIES

In the 1800s, some scientists believed Earth had once spun so fast that a large chunk broke off. They thought this chunk became the moon. However, Earth offers no proof it ever rotated this quickly.

Another **theory** was that the moon and Earth formed near each other at the same time from the same matter. However, while Earth and the moon share some matter, there are differences, too. For example, the moon doesn't have as much iron. Also, scientists think the moon is younger than Earth.

OUT OF THIS WORLD!

For many years, people believed that the Pacific Ocean covered the spot where the moon had broken off!

18

The idea that the moon came from a chunk of Earth is called the fission theory. "Fission" means "splitting apart."
The idea that Earth and the moon formed at the same time has many names, including the coformation theory.

THE CAPTURE THEORY

In the early 1900s, some scientists began to think that the moon was once a planet. They believed it was captured by Earth's gravity as it flew past. However, this theory has several flaws.

Earth's gravity isn't strong enough to capture something the size of the moon. It wouldn't have been able to slow down the moon quickly enough. The moon would have **collided** with Earth instead. The odds of the moon gently entering an orbit around Earth are very unlikely.

Most scientists now think the capture theory, as it's called, is highly unlikely. They think a moon speeding towards Earth would have caused a major collision.

21

ONE GIANT LEAP

On July 20, 1969, US astronauts Neil Armstrong and Edwin "Buzz" Aldrin became the first people to set foot on the moon. They **explored** one of the lunar maria called the Sea of Tranquility. Between 1969 and 1972, 12 astronauts walked on the moon.

The astronauts brought back about 2,200 moon rocks, weighing 842 pounds (382 kg). These samples were important clues in learning how the moon was formed. Rocks can tell the story of how moons and planets were made.

OUT OF THIS WORLD!

The astronauts wore space suits in order to walk on the moon. The suits provided air to breathe and kept them safe from the sun's harmful rays.

Astronauts used wheeled machines called rovers to travel many miles on the moon.

MOON MATERIAL

Scientists didn't know exactly what the moon was made of until the astronauts brought back rock and soil samples. The samples showed that the moon has rocks similar to those on Earth.

Volcanoes created most of the moon rocks. Rocks made of cooled lava are called igneous rocks. The lunar maria are made of igneous rocks called basalts. The lunar highlands are mostly made of igneous rocks called anorthosites. Basalts and anorthosites are found on Earth, too.

Lunar soil isn't really soil because there's nothing living in it. It's called regolith.

25

GIANT IMPACT THEORY

In the mid-1970s, scientists came up with the giant **impact** theory. This idea was that a planet the size of Mars slammed into Earth 4.5 billion years ago. The collision destroyed layers of Earth, sending magma and large pieces of both planets into space.

The **debris** orbited Earth in a clump and finally formed a ball of molten rock. This chunk cooled down and became the moon we see today. Most scientists agreed that this was the best explanation for how the moon was formed.

OUT OF THIS WORLD!

While the moon was still forming, many large **meteorites** hit it. That's how most of the moon's mountains and craters came to be.

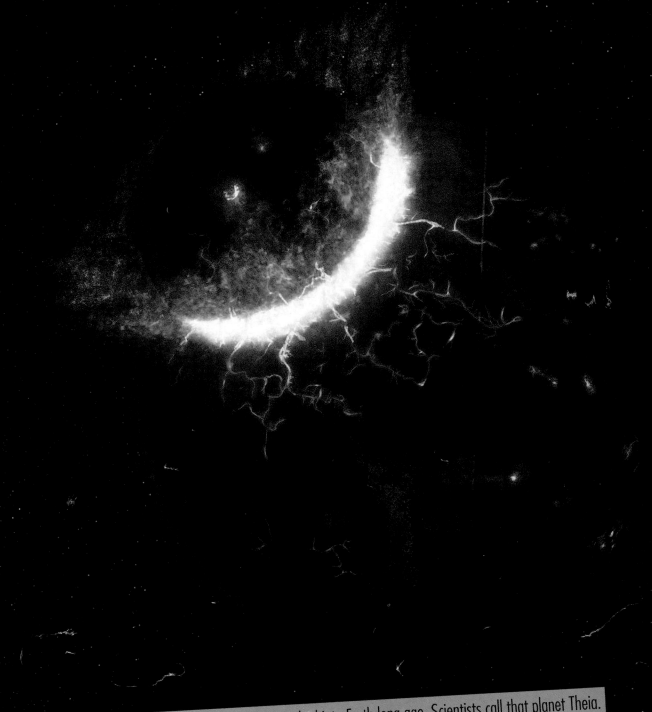

According to the giant impact theory, a planet smashed into Earth long ago. Scientists call that planet Theia.

MOON MYSTERY

Despite years of study, we still aren't entirely sure how the moon was formed. Recently, some scientists have suggested that the giant impact theory has flaws, too. If a collision did occur, both Earth and the moon should have pieces of the object that hit Earth. So far, scientists have been unable to find proof. They think that the moon could have formed from Earth alone.

One thing is certain. Much more exploration must be done to solve the mystery of how the moon was formed.

electric lunar rover

MOON FACTS

temperature range	−244°F (−153°C) to 273°F (134°C)
oldest rock found	4.5 billion years old
deepest crater	15,000 feet (4,572 m)
widest crater	140 miles (225 km)
speed of rotation	about 10 miles (16 km) per hour
orbit around Earth	once every 27 days, 7 hours, 43 minutes

While there are currently landing crafts exploring the surface of Mars, there are no crafts exploring the surface of the moon. More exploration might give us more answers.

GLOSSARY

astronomer: a person who studies stars, planets, and other heavenly bodies

collide: to crash

debris: the remains of something that has been broken

explore: to search in order to find out new things

gravity: the force that pulls objects toward the center of a planet, star, or moon

impact: the action of one thing hitting another

lava: hot, liquid rock that flows from a volcano or from a crack in a planet or moon

magma: hot, liquid rock inside a planet or moon

meteorite: a space rock that has reached the surface of a moon or planet

solar system: the sun and all the space objects that orbit it, including the planets and their moons

telescope: a tool that makes faraway objects look bigger and closer

temperature: how hot or cold something is

theory: a set of ideas meant to explain something

FOR MORE INFORMATION

BOOKS

Mitton, Jacqueline. *Moon*. New York, NY: DK Publishing, 2009.

Slade, Suzanne. *The Phases of the Moon*. New York, NY: PowerKids Press, 2007.

Winrich, Ralph. *The Moon*. Mankato, MN: Capstone Press, 2008.

WEBSITES

Ask a Lunar Scientist
lunarscience.nasa.gov/ask-a-scientist/
Do you have a question about the moon? See if it's answered on this site.

The Earth's Moon
www.kidsastronomy.com/earth/moons.htm
Read about the moon and learn other fun facts about the solar system.

INDEX